MOTIVATION

Unique and Definitive Planning of All Successful Professional Sellers

Use the information under your own risk.

Motivation and Movements EN MI©

**Dedicated to my father
I always be inspirited by
his ability to negotiate.**

Index of Contents

Contents

Embrace Love

Movement Model – Start Movement

Day One: Monday

Day Two: Viable - Expectative – Day Three: Motivation

Questions of the Movement Model

Day three: Motivation

Day four: Numbering and write

Day five: Illusion

Day six: My focus

Day Seven: Start to LOVE

Exercise Movement Model

Exercise: Movement In Me

Conclusion

Bibliography

Introduction

This book was written with the intention of motivate all the people who want to sell.

Selling is one of the most fascinating professions and we must motivate ourselves everyday to be a successful seller.

The motivation is one of the most energetic forces that a human can have in any work that begins.

The most motivated seller in the world is happy with his work and with everything that entails a sale in any field.

Motivate ourselves to sell can make our day special and happy.

The sale

The sale as a profession is considered as a very lucrative profession especially when we are motivated and we love the profession of selling.

When we sell we communicate our ideas and the customer receives the benefit of our product or service.

Sell is visiting the customers and show them all the benefit, keeping the order established by providing the service timely with responsibility of the both parts.

The personality of the seller must be friendly and with a motivation of consent present in every moment and the most important thing, the seller must be honest in what relates to his product, the seller can't trick his customers.

Motivation for a seller

For a seller, the motivation is very important because a seller must always have inspiration to keep going and to have success in the sales.

In this book we will motivate ourselves to sell and especially we will learn some important tools that will help us to convert our motivation into efficient sales.

The motivation is when we have a strong desire of doing something as we explain it in the movement model with the word "intensity".

A seller must focus in the enthusiasm that can be put when a service or a product is offer. The seller must feel with the energy to offer the best of him to do optimal sales.

When a seller is motivated with the movement model that is explained in one of the chapters of this book, the planning of selling will be so effective that the sales will increase in a high percentage, you will notice the different between the before and the after when you read this book.

It is important that as a seller we find the capital reason to sell our product or service, in this case with the right planning and the right model we will not postpone the things that we must do but we will use the motivation and the right movement to accomplish our goals with the sales.

We will learn that our time is precious and we will use it in the right way.

A seller must always have a positive attitude, as it happens with an interview, the first words and the first seconds are decisive in a sale.

A seller that is considered professional must know the mission and the vision of the product.

The seller must learn new things every day and must be update with new motivation and desire to achieve the goal.

A seller must be specialized in the product, must know it, love it and care about it.

And the most important thing is that the professional ethic must be real and constant.

Selling is the process in which a person helps other to make the decision of buying something. The emotional bond and the empathy between the seller and the buyer are very important.

The motivation in the sales is very important because it give us the energy and the impulse to sell our products and to go through all the obstacles and the problems that can appear.

The motivation can be for

Successful sales

Recuperate a client

Find a new client

The motivation for any of these options is the best thing to a motivated seller.

Values

Motivation In Me Model

M =

O =

T =

I =

V =

A=

T=

I=

O=

N=

I=

N=

M=

 E=

L

O

V

E

When we sell we must visit our client and show them the benefit of our product or service.

A motivated seller must have knowledge of everything that involves the selling process and also must have specific qualities.

1.   Help the clients in every moment.

2.   A lot of energy and motivation to work.

3.   Knowledge of everything that involves the product or service.

4.   Organization of the time, movements of selling and personal life.

The attitude must be always positive.

The personality of the seller must go always focus to the optimism of the work.

The attitude expresses the feelings and the thoughts of the seller. With a motivated attitude the seller transmits confidence.

The dedication to the profession in every sense is the motto of the most motivated seller.

Think and act like the most motivated seller in the world.

Your attitude is going to determinate your way of seeing the life.

Motivating Communication

The communication is an exchange of thoughts, opinions, ideas and information through speech. The communication is verbal and nonverbal.

The motivation of the seller: The motivation can push the people to work harder for achieve their goals.

The movements of the seller are equivalent to the motivation.

Movement = Motivation

IN ME   IN ME

The motivation moves you everyday to achieve the goals that you have.

The motivation is a powerful force for our life.

With the right motivation we are going to be:

1. Positives

2. Accurate

3. Auto disciplined

4. Enthusiastic

5. Friendly

6. Energy

7. Interest

8. Initiative

9. Accurate movements

10. Inspiration to do everything that you proposed

11. Love every movement.

Motivation in Me

In this book you are going to motivate yourself and to believe in your own potential for the sales by follow the movement and motivation model. The inspiration is very important to make your sales achieve the desired goal. With the correct inquiry you are going to detect what is moving you to sell. The positive though while you're doing your sales will be an optimistic forward every day.

The imagination as an important part of the model will help you to advance in the achieving of your goals.

The responsibility (IN ME) that you have to the motivation and that your goals become a reality depends on you as a "seller". If you are the most motivated seller in the world, please repeat 5 times "I'm the most motivated seller in the world".

The responsibility that you must implement to start loving the movement model will give you the strength to know that you are the responsible of your life and also of the motivation that you will put in your sales.

The motivation of imagine so many sales will have positive results; the motivation must be developed to increase our sales.

The good sale is to sell as a natural habit of our life.

The positive attitude makes us see any problem in a nicer way.

Marketing

In the world of the sales the marketing where I'm working is very important for the planning and the motivation that I have to do my sales.

Marketing is a tool that every seller must know.

All companies in some way use techniques of marketing, even without knowing. Marketing is only the exchange between a minimum of 2 parts so a mutual benefit occurs.

Most people believe that marketing (or market which would be its literal translation into Spanish) consist in do advertising (often in an "unethical" way) to indiscriminately sell a product to any user who is exposed to an advertisement or a promotion campaign.

Most marketers and business advisers should clarify that marketing includes advertising as one of its components, but it is much more.

Most modern companies have a classified department with the specific functions that are associated with this activity.

The marketing is framed from the point of view of its final results, which are none other than the needs and demands of consumers, and therefore, to sell.

Likewise it is not easy a definition of "marketing" it is not easy a typology of this discipline according to a certain criterion.

A good marketing analysis should take into account the objectives, the strategies developed to achieve these objectives, and both internal and external business environment is studied.

It is the set of activities by various means (mail, television, and direct mail), products or services that had been previously defined into market segments are offered to potential consumer to obtain a direct response.

The 4 P of marketing

Product: are the goods and services offered to consumers in order to meet their needs.

What does the customer want from our product or service?

What does the customer need from the product? What characteristic has to have the product to satisfy their needs?

Price:

The monetary value of a product according to its application, quality, distribution, discounts, rebates, guarantees to potential consumers.

What value has the product or service to the customer? Are there standard prices established?

Place:

It is the path and location that a product takes as it moves through the market, channel or path. It includes the producer and consumer, locations, transportation, storage, offices.

Where your customers searched product or service? What kind of store or trade? How to access to the right channels of distribution?

Promotion

It is the set of techniques developed by companies to publicize their products or services to consumers so that they would be boosted to buy them.

Through advertising, sales, personal, promotions, display, electronic sales.

Where and when communicate messages to the target customer? What is the best time to make promotion? How the competition does the promotion?

Objection

In the world of the sales it is important to know that in some cases my motivation could wane just because I don't know how to answer an objection of a customer and because of that the mutual motivation, between the customer and I, must be always at 100 %.

Overcoming Objections

To overcome an objection can remove a barrier in the purchase. What the potential customer is really saying is "I would buy it, but…" The following are ways for you to overcome objections:

.You can paraphrase the objection to make sure that you have properly heard what you customer said. Use a closed question to check that you captured the subject and you understood it well. The best way is to make your sentences begin with "so what you want to know is …".

.Provide information to appease the matter, and when it is possible illustrate the point with some additional benefit.

.Use a closed question to make sure that your potential customer is now comfortable and ready to do an order.

In many cases the objections serve to sell faster our product or service. If you don't want to have many problems with the objections

1.   Face it

2.   Know your product or service

3.   Listen carefully

4.   Stay calm

5.   The energy should transmit security

6.   Try to reduce their objections to a minimum

You must be prepared for all the objections and you must be able to handle them with the intelligence of a good seller, the motivation will help us to face them.

Objections

1. Respect the other's point of view

2. Understand the issue well

3. Confirm with a closed question

4. Use tools of illustration

5. Think before you answer

6. Bring testimonials

7. Accept that you can be wrong

Territory - Transmit- Telemarketing
Territory

The territory sets everything that I have to do to achieve my goal, I must study the territory and segment it while I'm organizing my strategic planning with the movement model.

Transmit

It is important the message that we transmit so the customer can understand our product or service.

Often are more important the emotions that we transmit than the message that we are giving. So we must transmit positive energy and optimism while we are doing our sales demonstrations.

We must transmit a faint smile of acceptance of our service or product.

Telemarketing It is important to make calls to arrange appointments when is necessary.

Organize and write.

Initiative and information

The initiative is very important in the world of sales because if we are motivated the initiative of each being comes in addition, the initiative is reflected in the beginning of our sale and the information we have in our product, our customer, our territory, our market etc.

The more information we have in our product and our customers, any effort that we should make to achieve the sale will flow instantly.

You must know the information of the competition and you always must offer the correct information.

Find out everything related to the sale.

Information

Sales

The sale is our goal and we will achieve it with the movement and motivation model because these two models have motivated us to achieve all the goals set on the sale of our product or service.

Get orders

Short deadlines

Profit of the seller

Good communication

Stages

The life cycle of a product is divided into four stages. Each phase corresponds to a trend of sales of that product

Introduction stage

Growth stage

Mature stage

Decline stage

Introduction Stage

This stage marks the beginning of the life of the product or service. During this stage, the benefits of the product to the company are minimal. The sales are very low and not even enough to cover their costs of production and marketing.

The product is not yet known, so the company must invest heavily in promotion and advertising.

At this stage, the company must calibrate very well the degree of implementation which aims to achieve and invest what is necessary to get the desired benefits with the new product or service.

The cost of producing the unit is high, thus input prices are also often high.

Many times the performance of the product is negative but you should insist investing money for customers.

Growth stage

When the product begins to be accepted in the market, the sales start to grow and you will start to see the benefits, yet in a slowly way.

Manufacturing costs are reduced (For more experience in production, or by a higher volume of production) and the incomes grow beyond the expenses, which tend to stabilize.

However, many companies choose to maintain a high price. Promotion and advertising are very important to publicize the brand image in the market and achieve the need of the product among the users.

Mature stage.

There comes a time when the product already has a market and the sales finally reach their highest level. The product demand, between permanent and occasional customers, normalizes and the costs continue to decline.

In principle, and if everything has developed normally, the resources are high and the company begins to collect their profits without reinvesting.

Decline stage

Given the market saturation, some competitors and also substitutes products will appear.

The benefits can become lost and the sales begin its descent, so should take actions on this.

What we have seen so far is the theory of the stages of the product; the life of a product or service, but the reality may be different.

And even more in modern times.

Value - Values

The values that we have as a person are very important for our sale to become a success. In our model we will talk more about this topic with some questions to know and to strengthen our values. But we will focus even more in the valuation at everything related to our sale, that added value that we must have in all of our actions.

The value of learning for a seller is very important because it takes his career to another level. When you learn subconsciously you start practicing all the valuable knowledge you acquire so your movements will be inspirational and motivational in order to become the world's most motivated seller.

In this issue we must highlight that the emotional value for a purchase is even more important than the need of the product or service, according to studies of emotional topic. (Intelligence)

The added value is tangible and intangible

Tangibles

Free samples

Advertising

Journals – Magazine

Intangible: Business Roundtable, personal development courses, invitations to events.

Later we will see an exercise of Values.

Assertiveness + Agreement + amplification + answer

It is a communicational behavior in which the person is not aggressive and is subject to the will of others, but expresses the own convictions and defends the own rights. That is, knowing that when you communicate with the customer you are not hurt or harm him, and you are not communicating with anger and anxiety.

It is a new term that is important in the process of the sales.

Many authors believe that assertiveness is synonymous with social skills and other authors consider that assertiveness is only a part of social skills.

I agree with the second group because social skills cover many other aspects.

Always give the reason to the other person doesn´t mean to be assertive because we can and we should express our opinion even if it is right or not. In the case of the sales being assertive means express our opinions respecting our customers.

Agreement

All days we are doing agreements, with our client it is vital for a good negotiation.

Amplification

We must amplify everything on our expertise in sales and development of our profession so every day we expand our minds and be more open to learning and update us in many aspects such as technology. Amplify as the word says is ample, in this case we must focus on expanding our knowledge, our relationships, our emotional intelligence, our inspiration, our techniques, our gratitude, our attitude, our responsibility, our order, our imagination, our innovation our optimism and our movement model. Amplify on the good sense of increasing wealth and all that is required for optimal performance in one of the most beautiful profession on the planet earth as the sales.

Answer Prepare good answers for anticipating your client.

Obtain Answers

The answer given by the client of our product or service is telling us if they like it or don't it like. It is important to capture the emotionality in their answers to understand the degree of appreciation of our product or service.

The answers that we provide to the questions of our customers are fundamental to the success of our sales.

The motivation that we use when we express these words will affect the degree of acceptance of our product and the continuity of our customer.

The 9C: Customer, Communication, Continuity, Connection, Confident, Conscious, Close, Control, Calm

This is a secret of my experiences with the sales.

I've sold from perfumes, jewelry, furniture, real estate, insurance, advertising... to sports entertainment, aluminum and everything related. I mean, I´ve sold many products and services, and I´m sure that if you follow this 9Ctechnique, you will have a successful sale.

Customer

The customer is very important for the sale and all the success of a satisfactory sale is focus on the customer. We always will have a direct contact with our customer while we are doing a sale.

We must be close to our customer with an extensive knowledge of what he really wants so we can offer an optimal product or service.

We should have a list of our customers, a file where we are going to organize the customers according to their territory.

It is important that when we are following the movement model we take notes of all related to our possible customer or to our customer. It is vital to follow our relationship with the customer even after the sale is done.

We must listen, see, serve and understand our customer.

The customer is the raison of existence of a business or service focused on sales.

Customers and their types

The one who is not decided: the customer who just listens and has an impenetrable face. You have to ask to make him talk.

The speaker: Set the dialogue and learn to listen without interrupting.

The questioner: when the customer asks, awaits for your response. Also, if he is making questions is because he is interested in purchasing.

The one who likes to discuss: If the customer likes to discuss is waiting that you give him a consistent reason, not a reason of compromise. Use your skills to insinuate something and try to look like it is the client´s idea, but do not argue.

The shy: He is the one that doesn´t dare to decide. Requires gentleness and not aggressiveness; understanding and trust, because he is afraid to make mistakes.

The one who is expanding: Take the initiative of the conversation and return to the sale, because it can be a very long interview and we can not just lose that sale, but others that are waiting. The time required restraint.

The one who is not focus: You should be careful about if he is paying attention. Ask him if he is worry about the product. Return to the topic of the product so he can participate in the conversation.

The one who doesn´t trust: He has doubts about the product, and he doesn´t trust in your words, but if you know well the product you will overcome his objections.

The variable: He doesn´t know what he wants: changes his opinions and needs help and approval.

The grumpy: He can be grumpy or act like one. Be attentive, helpful and don´t be controversial. Warm smile and good mood.

Please, be nice.

The communicative: his conversation is very dominant and the sale does not materialize.

He can be expressive, nice and ingenious, but please return to your presentation.

Return to the sale.

The quiet: He is very quiet.

Using questions you can make that he talks and make sure that your presentation is serviced.

The one who is looking for rebates: looking for all kinds of discounts and rebates.

When the final price is present and the seller offers promotion prices in this point, that promotion is not credible.

Communication

The communication is a process that involves two or more people (emitters and receivers of the same message) and the means by which the idea is transmitted.

The tune is when is use a common language between the individuals.

When the language is common between the seller and the customer everything about the sale it is more efficient and fluid.

Remember that are part of the communication:

The gestures

The body and its position

Contacts

The looks

Expressions

The client can be

Visual

They are the customers who want to look at the price, see the product, a report that they can see, see the results, look at statistics and see graphs.

Their expressions are generally

See, look, dark, light, observe.

Hearing customers

They are customers who prefer to communicate through the sounds of their listening.

Their expressions are Talk, express, say, listen.

Sensory customers

Predominantly communication through gestures, body language and looks

Their expressions are strong, feel, balance, touch, pick.

Continuity

It is very important to follow your customers and this mean to have continuity, the continuity of our relationships with the customer for a good service.

The customers or clients must understand that when they are buying our service or product, the continuity of the relationship between the customer and the seller will continue till it is necessary.

Often the continuity can be with the same service or product o with a new one, depending on our offers.

With continuity I mean the continuity that I must have with my client. This follow up can be by telephone, mail, visits, Christmas cards, promotion information and new products or services.

In the model we express the starting, the love and the gratitude. Call your customer to give thanks for the purchase.

Continuity in customer service:

Excellent service, service before-during-Post sale, professional support, Compliance, Attention to the Customer complaints and claims, new orders

Connection

The connection we have with our client should be strongly influenced emotionality because it is an important factor for the customer to purchase of our product or service.

When the client understands the need and urgency to buy our product or service, it is the right way to close our sale, so we will understand that the connection between the seller and the client was optimal.

Confidence

The confidence that our customers feel for us is vital to sell our product or service, the customer gives us his confidence while we also trust him.

It is important when we have a high esteem to have also a high confidence in ourselves.

When we are sure of getting our sale and close the sale it is more likely that we had confidence in our product, our company and ourselves.

The trust we give to the customer is ultimately for the purchase of a product or service.

The most important thing is that you must have confidence in yourself.

Trust your qualities seller. If you follow the models in this book, you will surely acquire accurate and concise information to sell.

Here you have the guidelines needed to become the professional seller you want to be.

Conscious

Knowing everything about the sale is essential for the success of a professional seller.

I Always reiterate in this manual that it is very important to be conscious about everything related to sales.

From my conscious to the conscious of the client

Close: We deepen more in the technique on the movement model.

Control: In all my information and my sale.

Calm: Be calm in everything that relates with my sale.

Inquire - Image

Inquire (about the type of customer referent to the sale)

Inquire and investigate all that matters relating to the company or the customer that we have to convince for our future sale. When we are on the presentation we often inquire about the customer needs of our product or service.

Investigate all that matters relating to the response that we have to give to our customers so it becomes into a successful sale.

When we study, we analyze and we offer all with an excellent level we will secure and develop the expected success of our product or service.

You should investigate the market where you will work and get ready to find new customers.

Tips to find our client

1. Directories

2. Press

3. Catalogs

4. Internet

5. Referrals

6. List of the chamber of commerce

7. Neighbors

8. Customers

9. List of shopping malls.

Investigate technology. We should know the new technological concepts to advance with them.

For example, with the internet where the marketing can be exploited according to the needs of my product or service.

Image

So far, we have the general principle. However, this basic premise doesn't worth all the time because there are special, select or very regular customers. Sometimes, the company believes that it is worth investing all the time it takes to convince an unhappy customer - even knowing that is wrong - because the quality, prestige or frequency of purchase of the customer will make in the long run that this investment results beneficial to the company. In this case, it is very important to try to prove to the customer that we have not failed and support the quality and efficiency of our company in front of him. Once convinced, often we should offer alternatives to balance his initial discontent. The image is very important where attire and punctuality is included. Even professional business cards that show your personal brand will help.

I usually arrive 10 minutes before a sales appointment.

Obtain market and reflection

Obtain everything that we have proposed to ourselves. If we use correctly the time, the resources and everything that we have in our hands for our planning and our movements, we will get to the success of the sale of our product or service.

We should watch with interest what the customer is telling us because if we are focused we will resolve all the objections that arise with our clients. Reflection of all I´m doing with the sale and, if I´m doing the correct movements with this client.

Obtain Market

In the world of the sales the market where I'm working is very important for the planning and the motivation that I have to do for my sales. However effective and original is our advertising campaign, it is impossible to reach a market that we don't know well. The first step of a relationship is based on mutual understanding of the partners: tastes, interests, aspirations ... two strangers won't understand if they not previously known each other. The market has some homogeneous characteristics that we should know if we want to discover the reasons why customers are going to prefer us and not the competition. The company must define a target market and focus on that territory. The market is the identifiable group of consumers with a purchasing power that are willing to pay for a product or service.

Reflection

The word reflection is very important when we have not closed the sale and when we closed it. When we have not closed the sale we must think what we missed and what we must complement and express to our client to close the sale. If we close the sale the reflection is to use the tactics that we used in this sale and reflect on what we should improve.

Negotiate vs Sell

The process of negotiate is often confused with selling. When you negotiate you have to use so many of the techniques of the selling, but it is a much more complex process. The one who is negotiating is looking for the solution that meets the needs of the both parts – sometimes opposed-. Sales skills are needed for negotiators to focus their interactions so they can achieve commitments at each stage, until this agreement is successfully concluded.

Building relationships

Longer terms

Earn customer and sell

Sales Skill

Direct

In my demonstration – Empathy, Listen, interest

In my demonstration

In my demonstration is one of the most important aspects in the beautiful world of the sales. We could say that in this motivation model this demonstration would be art.

The seller must prepare the demonstration and everything that is related to the product for the day that he is going to offer it to his customers.

In this respect the movement model has an important and high charge for planning your visit of your sales and goals.

A good presentation should contain

1-Explanation of your product or service

2-Concept of our product or service

3-How it works

4-Benefits

5-Successful Closing of the Sale

Empathy

The empathy is very important because with this we can understand better the need of our customer and we can match in so many ways with them.

The empathy is essentially the ability to put yourself in the place of others, the ability to sense precisely the reactions, feelings and needs of our interlocutor.

The empathy involves the possibility of filing a fluid and constructive communication, through a sensitive and receptive attitude to the other.

An empathetic person can easily recognized the clues and cues that the listener offers so they can relate in an effective and rewarding way for both.

Listen: All the questions and objections of my client and wait at least 4 seconds to give him a good answer.

The interest includes the interest of qualify and educate ourselves to become a professional seller, so our emotionality flows through the positive and successful side of us.

Interest

The interest that we give to the client will influence largely on the success of our sale.

Keep our customer interested is vital for a happy and complete closure between the parts.

We must keep our customer interested by using all the means that offer the social networks and the internet so that incentive will become one benefit of all our proposals.

Listen

It is one of the most important to listen our client , in general we have to increase our listening for a good understanding with all persons.

Needs

We must find a need and make it a profit for what we are offering. We must listen and observe and so when we meet and detect our customer needs our product or service can be used to close a sale.

It is important to use the proper and necessary time to communicate and express what we offering with our product or service.

We summarize the needs that our product or service can solve for our client, and it is important that we express what we sense and understand of their needs so we can expose our summary with a question.

Movement Model

The initiation of the movement model is fundamental for a good sale in every way. If you wish to complement and reinforce the movement model you can buy the book Motivation.

We have reached one of the most important models to plan our goals correctly and complete.

The movement model has three phases: initiation, promotion and reinforcement.

We have focused on the beginning phase because we believe that with this guide you can become the most motivated and efficient seller of the world.

It is explain better in movement model.

Embrace to Love

Likable attitude

Long lasting customer

It is very important to continue with our client this means more and more sales.

With this model you organize your work better and

This means more and more sales.

Embrace Love

Start to love is one of the most important models of our motivation model as we had always explain it. We always must start to love our movements and our goals and in the beginning the continuity is essential because our love should not be reduced at any time.

Start to love is the work that I'm doing by using all these tools that I have such talents that I have not found that I have to use them towards my goals.

Own movement

Obtain Anticipation

The anticipation, as well as the word says, is that we must anticipate to the facts in this motivation model. It means anticipate the answers to the possible questions that can ask us our customer.

It is important to clarify that we must listen and never lose our focus from the next question that we will do to our customer.

Anticipation is preparing responses to be natural to respond to our customer so we must study them in advance to avoid falling into the trap of not knowing the answer.

.

Obtain Challenge

It is important to challenge me every day to get better and sell more and more.

Obtain Repeat

My 2 movement and motivation models.

Value your movements

Enlarge reflection

Every day I have to be efficient in my life and in my work.

Synthesis of the Motivation In Me Model

M = Marketing

O = Objection

T = Territory +Transmit + Telemarketing

I = Initiative + information

V = Values

A= Assertiveness +Agreement +amplification+ answer

T= the 9C Customer-Communication-Continuity-

Connection-Confident-Conscious-Close-Control-Calm

I= Inquire +Image

O= Obtain Market + reflection

N= Negotiation

I= In my : Demonstration, Empathy, Listen, Answer

N= Needs

M= Movement Model

E= Embrace Love

L= Likable attitude+ long lasting customer

O= Oobtain challenge+ anticipation + repeat

V= Value your movements

E= Enlarge reflection

Movement Model – Start Movement

Welcome to a model that will help you to plan your goal on 7, 14 and 21 days. If you apply it correctly it will change your life by just being able to accomplish this goal.

With this theory the goals are better planned every week so there is more chance of achieving it in a short, medium or long term.

We have focused on a planned target in one week to three weeks, but in fact the model can also be applied to plan your week with everyday tasks purpose.

The goal can be achieved in one week or you can review your movements that have been made to fulfill the goal every week.

When I say (IN ME) I mean every person that will be performing the model.

It may be a long goal but it's the person who decides whether Movement Impulse or Strengthening Movement.

It is a self-training.

Guide:

Prefer not to be part of the great number of people who prefer to continue ignoring their days in criticism, complaints, cynicism, inaction, simple survival.

This program is a great opportunity.

- Discover what is holding you back or hinders and what to do about it.

- Achieve your goals.

- Discover how to bring your mind to the fullest potential so you can create the results you want in your life.

- In this program you will find strategies and tools that are based on the science of how our mind and emotions work and how to use them to create the success we seek.

- It's time to believe in yourself.

- When you have the right tools anything is possible.

- Requires that you implement with determination, only then going to get the results you want.

- Connect daily with the movement. What it counts is the way of every movement.

- It is a model where the motivation and inspiration will be present all the time.

- The personal motivation will make you move every day.

- You will succeed to achieve and accomplish goals.

- Your life will change with the planning of your goal and you will achieve it.

I would like to congratulate you on the decision to buy this book

"Action is the proper fruit of knowledge" T. Fuller

- This movement model is an important tool to achieve and create the life you want and help others to also meet the success.

- Build a habit for the foundation necessary for your environment.

- Expand the clarity of your goals and how to reach them

-We'll have plenty of practice, so it will be a wonderful model.

Hint: Buy a notebook to perform the exercises.

It is a very special book work.

- A work book.

It is a method to go and perform a step or movement every day

You must memorize the following keys at every move

You will have 2 movements every day

1.   Start Movement

Please, learn in this way:

MO – Monday

VE – Tuesday

ME – Wednesday

NT – Thursday

IN – Friday

ME – Saturday

NOW – Sunday

You must know that you have 2 letters of the word MOVEMENT each day of the week.

So it is preferable to start on Monday but not indispensable.

The method is explained to begin on Monday if the person changes should only write the 2 syllables in the first day.

Example beginning Tuesday:

Tuesday – MO

Wednesday – VE

Thursday – ME

Friday – NT

Saturday – IN

Sunday – ME

Monday – NOW

It is easier to memorized starting on Monday and also the example of the book is always starting on Monday.

The person will know that they are two syllables each day.

Even to remember in a better way you can be guided by the Wednesday. The 2 syllables are always ME

Example

Monday

Tuesday

Wednesday ME

Intelligence: Increase your intelligence, think, read, several solutions to a goal.

Emotional intelligence is the human capacity to feel, understand, control and modify emotional states in oneself and in others. Emotional intelligence is not to stifle emotions, but direct them and balance them. It involves the totality of psychological skills that allow us to appreciate and express our emotions, understand the emotions of the others, and use this information to guide our thinking and behavior.

The movement model allows

Learn about relationships with the model

Models for efficiency

Strengthen skills in me

Expansion

Exercise me

You first enter to the world of the movement model.

The goal is something that you want to make in short, medium and long term.

The objectives are specific and you can achieve them by following a list of steps.

It is important to note that sometimes I'm reinforcing the concepts.

For two reasons in particular

1-   For the model to be understood.

2-   A specific technique of the model

Exercise

Pick five sales goals you want to achieve and write them

1.

_____

_____

_____

_____

_____

_____

2_____

_____

_____

_____

_____

_____

3.

_____

_____

_____

_____

_____

4._____

_____

_____

_____

_____

Questions in my model

1. What do you want to take your life to another level?

2. Why is this so important?

3. Who are you? Describe yourself

4. What are your values?

5. What is your goal? From the biggest to the smallest

1._____

_____

2._____

_____

3._____

_____

4._____

_____

5._____

_____

Learning

Skill becomes natural behavior - until you feel it can be done naturally.

WHERE IT HAPPENS
THE LEARNING

Unconscious Competence

Conscious Competence

Unconscious Incompetence

Conscious Incompetence

It is important that everything you do on the week to achieve your goal becomes natural.

That is, each day I propose to do everything that is in my hands in order and with the thought of victory in my goal.

We go beyond

With the planning of my goal my life will move to another level.

It is important to clarify that this model is auto-training, so you must do the exercises with the help of the book.

There are many professionals that can help you to achieve your goal and this is also very valid too.

There are many professionals that have this purpose and have optimal results.

Remember that even if this method is self training you can also be accompanied by a professional trainer.

Advancing in our skills

We learn about our creativity and leadership to bring our lives to the next level.

It may be that some of the concepts you'll find in this method will be repetitive, it is very important an attitude of "Your can view this from a different perspective in particular you will see it as part of a system of personal development and as a tool that will serve you to improve your life in any field, it's just a seed of training for increasingly more progress"

When we are open to learning and to take our knowledge to another level

Advancing in my seed

- Risks: all involves a risk

- Creativity: the goal should complement our creativity

- Goals: choose five goals and develop one

- Leadership: leadership that goal

- We will achieve that goal.

Exercise

Write what is motivating me to make goals

In my seed

Start Movement

MONDAY – MO Corresponds to the words

My goal

Organization

TUESDAY – VE Corresponds to the words

Viable

Expectative

WEDNESDAY – ME Corresponds to the words

Motivation

Entrepreneurship

THURSDAY – NT Corresponds to the words

    Numbering

    To write

Start to love

    FRIDAY – IN Corresponds to the words

Illusion+ introduction of priority

New technique

    SATURDAY - ME Corresponds to the words

    My focus

    Embrace love

SUNDAY – Corresponds to the words

    I like it and I start to love

Likable attitude

Own movements

Value your movements with responsibility

Enlarge gratefulness and efficien

MO – Monday

VE – Tuesday

ME – Wednesday

NT – Thursday

IN – Friday

ME – Saturday

NOW – Sunday

M = My goal

. O = Organization

. V = Viable

. E = Expectative

. M = Motivation

. E = Entrepreneurship + Emotions

. N = Numbering

. T = To write

. S= Start to love

. I =Illision+ Introduction of priority

. N = New technique

. M = My focus

. E= Embrace love

.

. L = Likable attitude

. O = Own movements

. V = Value your movement with responsability

. E = Enlarge gratefulness and efficient

Start Movement

My goal –

Choose the goal

Organize everything around the goal to start and establish a viable order. The goal should be:

The goal of my sales must be clear

Arrange everything related to sales.

Organization

Organize

1-Time (Your Day)

2-Visits

3-Customers

4-In my presentation

5-Objections

6-Model Motivation

7-Model Movement

The goal is what we want to be fulfilled in short, medium or long term.

My purposes may vary in:

1. Personal

2. Family

3. Professional

4. Labor

With the movement pattern I can plan achievable goals that I propose because every day I realize at least two movements with the right motivation to work hard and achieve my dreams.

Viable

It means achievable.

My goal should be viable to be reachable.

The viability of my goal is very important because if it is an unattainable goal it will be very difficult to achieve that particular goal.

Expectative: I can imagine what is my expectative for my goal already accomplished.

The expectative also refers to all I can plan and structure for achieving the goal.

I must imagine in the first place all I will sell so I can always improve.

I should have the expectative of being the most motivated seller of the world and this will help me to grow.

Motivation

I should have a high motivation so every day I can make a move. The motivational book helps me a lot to increase my motivation every day.

To the most motivated seller in the world.

http://www.amazon.com/Motivaci%C3%B3n-
Alcanzar-inspiraci%C3%B3n-vida-Logra-
sue%C3%B1os-%C2%A1-
ebook/dp/B00RDWHVBY/ref=sr_1_2?ie=UTF8&
qid=1438811532&sr=8-2&keywords=motivacion

Entrepreneurship: You can also call it
"Innovation". It refers to the methodology that will
be used for achieve the goal. I must think of
something new that I have not done so far to reach
the goal.

I should have entrepreneurship and innovation in
my sales techniques.

The innovation is very fashionable these days

Innovation means introducing new change things. When we innovate in sales is important to think in terms of the progression of time.

To increase sales is important to innovate, with innovation the number of customers, sales and repeat sales will increase.

Motivation is the key to innovation in the field of sales for the customer and for the seller.

Numbering

It refers especially to numbering dates where you think you are going to realize the goal.

It is tangible numbers, use tools as calendars and figures if you require it.

You must write numbers that you have prospected to sell.

You should also number dates for the most important movements that you have to do to achieve the goal.

Numbers play an important role as the numbers specify a date or a value and thus will make more easily achieve our goal.

To write

You have to write your program of sales goals.

Write the steps that I can and I must perform in order that my goal becomes a reality.

Write everything I am doing.

Write everything about my client and in general with my product or service.

Including the writing of the emotions that I can feel when I'm making my moves and when it comes to sales. I should write the emotions that the client passed me while I convey emotions that my client.

You have to write new ideas.

Emotions

Emotions are an important step in the wonderful world of the sales because all human beings are emotional while all human beings are sellers.

We must learn to manage our emotions especially when we alter our emotions and this doesn't let us act in a successful manner.

The positive metal attitude plays an important role in our emotions and how we develop our emotional intelligence in particular. Our Star to love model will help us in the emotional aspect.

Start to love our positive and pleasant emotions.

New technique

It means that I have to look a very personal technique to motivate me so I can make the movement of the day (Book motivation).

The selling techniques are:

Closing techniques

There are so many techniques or tricks to help us to close the sale as there are as sellers.

Each seller has his own professional and personal behavior

Illusion

You can also call it "Optimism". It refers that this word should be a constant word so you can perform all the daily movements of the goal.

The most motivated seller in the world should always be optimistic and don't lose the illusion.

http://www.amazon.com/MOTIVACI%C3%93N-Autoestima-Psicolog%C3%ADa-Positiva-espiritual-ebook/dp/B00PPXK3O0/ref=sr_1_2?ie=UTF8&qid=1419367428&sr=8-2&keywords=motivacion+personal

New technique

This technique aims to prevent that the client doubt if he stays with the product or service. It is clear that he is going to stay with the product or service.

It's about understanding what he is going to keep exactly. For this, we go offering alternatives that allow them to be the real protagonist of his decisions.

These alternatives would serve to the seller to present the sale in a better way. I suggest to give them the option to choose between different sizes or quantities of a product or two different products that allow us to advise that "the one that fits your needs is"...

Technique

This technique seeks to show the client how lucky he was for being interested in buying our product in this moment, not before or after, as it is now when you have the precise circumstances to make a special offer, is unique and it is not repeatable if you buy now.

The seller can also make use of this technique during the objections, but there is a substantial difference.

When we try to answer the objections of the customer, we can use this technique only indirect and subtle way to prevent that our future client, still undecided, feels pressured.

At the close of the sale, we must mention to the buyer directly and specifying the "Good opportunity" that exists.

Presumably now the client is already predisposed to buy and what we want is to shift his attention from the purchase itself and focus it on secondary factors, such as the benefit that such product or service is going to offer and how he can take advantage of it.

My focus

It means that I should focus on the goal and I must concentrate hard on that goal so my movements should be focused on that purpose.

Focus on my goal.

Focus is a very important word. When we focus on what we want and if our essence is focused perfectly with that we probably achieve our goals.

The goals will always be focused on start loving our movements, our profession and all matters relating to the sale of our product or service.

Extra refers to the new movement of every day especially with the new prospects of the way in how I'm doing new movements. My movement must be renewed and accurate.

Everything must be done with new and extra ideas.

New is a word that indicates something newly created or manufactured. In the sales process if I find new customers, new concepts, new products, new services, means I'm moving in my movement.

For example the technology advances more and increasingly often with new products.

We must be updated in technology because also the world of sales is advancing with the technology.

I like it means that I will always like more and more the movements that I'm realizing to reach the goal.

Start to LOVE

I like sales.

Like it is a term that we use every day in our life and we should increasingly more like the movements we do to continue the beautiful way of life.

If we raise our morning and we reflect as we like our planet, our universe, our life, our profession, our family and everything that surrounds us today will be a certainly more harmonious and happy day.

Start to LOVE is the most important movement, this are the movements of the seventh day.

Start to love the sales in all its forms is fascinating.

I always have a likable attitude

Own movement means that my constancy in my movement should not decrease.

When we have this positive attitude this will influences the positive attitude that we have toward the product and to our company and to our client therefore we must be convinced that we will achieve the goal so our mind will be started positively and will be reflected in confidence and quiet.

It is important to remember that as well as achieving happiness can be learned our attitude optimistic too.

Martin Seligman, formulated the thesis called "Learned Optimism"

Value your movements with responsibility

It refers to giving thanks every day for the wonderful day and that good attitude. We should value that this attitude is maintained.

Always be grateful for my past, present and future sales.

Thanks for all the wonderful things that are happening to me. And with a lot of responsibility.

Thank is always an important word in our daily repertoire and certainly our appreciation will be reflected in our world and so this attitude of gratitude and love for everything around me will be a new world in me.

Efficient

It means that this model or method is an efficient way to improve my life and follow the movements for the realization of the goal.

The efficiency and the responsibility are very important things in everything related to the client and in my product or service.

The responsibility is a value which is in the consciousness of people and this allows direct its actions.

The responsibility for our actions and in this case the way we sell and our methodology will impact positively to the advancement of your career.

Enlarge gratefulness

It refers to giving thanks every day for the wonderful day and that good attitude. We should value that this attitude is maintained.

Always be grateful for my past, present and future sales.

Thanks for all the wonderful things that are happening to me. And with a lot of responsibility.

Thank is always an important word in our daily repertoire and certainly our appreciation will be reflected in our world and so this attitude of gratitude and love for everything around me will be a new world in me.

Start Movement. Day one

Day One:

On this day we will begin our methodology with the acronym Movement In Me. It is a movement of each person.

M My goal, Movement

O Organization, Order

As a exercise we write the goal as each time we will have a movement for the realization of our goal.

I write my goal and I organize everything I have to do this week for the realization of my goal.

It is very important to acquire a routine so we will not postpone anything. I'm going to have a discipline.

It is important to organize our time and use it well

1.   Organize the customers (Database)

2.   Write it all

3.   Use maps

4.   Investigate parking

5.   Classifieds

6.   Sort your customers for their interest in buying

7.   Investigate the direction ahead

8.   Punctuality primarily

What does the movement model

One of the most important steps is to explore who you are as a person to explore this we must ask the following questions.

1. Who are you?

2. What are your beliefs and values?

3. What is it that you defend?

4. What is the real purpose for which you do what you do?

Answering these questions brings you closer to your self-awareness and your self-discovery.

The confident that you give to yourself is vital for the training process

Definition

We will find many definitions of personal effectiveness. It is characterized by empowerment in people to create the life they desire.

We usually focus on growth and the achievement of the goals.

- It is self-discovery

- Bring my life to another level

- A Conversation power

Movement Model

The value of a model is to strengthen the ability to remember which are key components in a system or process.

Movement Model

Day 1 Monday

M=My goal

O=Organization

Day 2 Tuesday

V=Viable

E=Expectative

Day 3 Wednesday

M=Motivation

E=Entrepreneurship

Day 4 Thursday

N=Numbering

T=To write

S start to love

Day 5 Friday

I=Introduction of priority

N=New technique

Day 6 Saturday

M=My focus

E=Embrace love

Day 7 Sunday

L= Likable attitude

O= Own movements

V= Value your movements with responsability

E= Efficient + Enlarge gratefulness

The relationship with myself

You and you

Questions:

1. What do you want to know about the movement?

_____

_____

_____

_____

_____

2. How is this going to help you to be more effective and get the best out of yourself?

_____

_____

_____

_____

_____

3. What do you think are your challenges in your path to your achievement?

_____

_____

_____

_____

4. What skills are you going to use?

_____

_____

_____

_____

We can watch ourselves.

We focus on watching how we can improve and apply every day to achieve our goal.

Exercise

Some questions to know me better

_____

_____

_____

_____

I write what I think and what is my most important movement today.

In my movement

Seed in me

_____

_____

_____

_____

_____

Questions of the Movement Model

MO= My goal + organization

1.	Choose an area of your life that you have it as goal to accomplish.

2.	How would it be the situation for your purpose? Ideal?

3.	What will I arrange for my goal today?

4.	If I think that I will be ordained in my goal. How would be such a system?

An example:

Let's get started with the Monday

That day is

MO = My goal + organization + order.

VE = Viability + Expectative

I'm writing and suggesting you that you should start on Monday, but start a different day is not important but you have to write it to your best planning of the goal.

You can even start anytime but is a suggestion to begin Monday for a greater compliance of the goals.

Day Two:

On this day two I will verify the viability of my goal and that is whether it is feasible to perform.

Order:

On this day we will begin to have more ability to ask questions and our curiosity is increasingly open according to our process of self training. We will be found the answers for many doubts that we had in our lives.

The consciousness that opens in us is one of the most important experiences for our lives because we identify what we really want.

Note also that the customer would notice everything and every detail, however insignificant it may seem, and this can destroy our professional image to the prospective buyer.

The desk, the corresponding chairs, telephone, fax, computer, necessary documentation (brochures, posters, print ...), must be all with order and cleanliness, because this is the outward sign of the professionalism of the seller

Summary

From this day you will open your mind to the imagination.

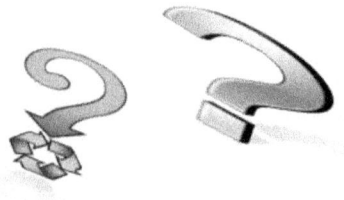

It means that we open our minds to what they are experiencing, feeling, seeing and believing.

Now, as you go on your way to becoming a better and better person:

Give yourself (a) the same feeling of compassionate exploration and curiosity about your own experiences. Be willing and then give yourself permission to explore the unknown with curiosity for learning.

Especially because when you are exploring this new world of movement now, it is important to find parts and moments that can challenge you, that will draw you from your comfort zone. Remember something that you have learned, but now you know naturally and comfort. On the way of learning you can make mistakes.

What is your experience when someone curious interacts with you? In these interactions you can feel:

- A natural desire and inclination to communicate openly.
- Creativity and imagination.

- Increased conscious of yourself and your potential
  It is in this climate that the conscious expands and the learning occurs

Start
Opportunity
View
Movement
Technical and Strategy

Feedback reviewing the results
Type of questions

- Open: Questions that invite the person to an open and free response of a definitive answer.

- In Me: Very effective questions that lead people to look at their issues with movement and transformation.

- Simple questions to reach the MOVEMENT IN ME

The importance of starting
The importance of investigating is attributable to all human beings and that curiosity is innate.
We have noticed, we have heard and we have realized that with all the inquiry we are going to get to the more intuitive and accurate questions.

Some of the steps to the success of my goal

a) Define what you want
b) Viable
c) Motivation
d) Technique
e)enumerate

Define (meaning) that is to direct your goal when you start practicing.

Values

A list of some values

- Happiness
- Bless you
- Joy
- Passion
- Connection
- Compassion
- Creativity
- Growth
- Freedom
- Adventure
- Achievement
- Contribution
- Power

- Money
- Spirituality
- Free time
- Family life
- Independence

List some other values that are important to you

- _____
- _____
- _____
- _____

My fundamentals values are:

- _____
- _____
- _____
- _____

According to the Dr. Demartini method we have these questions

1. How do you spend your time?

_____

_____

_____

2. How do you invest your energy?

_____

_____

_____

3. How do you invest your money?

_____

_____

_____

4. What is that thing that is always in your mind?

_____

_____

5. What do you visualize and what do you expect?

_____

_____

_____

_____

6. What inspires you the most?

_____

_____

_____

_____

Questions

"The quality of our questions determines the quality of our life. Successful people make better questions and as a result they get better answers"

Anthony Robbins

Exercise
Tuesday:

Questions of the Movement Model Viable, Expectative

1.   What is the feasibility of my goal?

2.   Is it true that I am aware of what I have to do to fulfill my goal?

3.   Is it true that my vision will be 100% for me to achieve this goal?

4.   My goal should be specific and it is feasible?

Everything around us will influence our behavior.

The goals are the aspirations that we have so we will take action to comply them. We should plan our goals with this book in 21 days. You should do 2 moves each day. Is easy, just 2 moves. It is like 2%, calculated on 1% per move.

I am giving you the steps to make the move. There is a reinforcement movement that you can realize after 14 days for completion of the movement of the day.

You have to accommodate your time depending if your goal is short, medium or long term.

Day three:

In this third day you will perform and discover how to move forward with your goal and you will find innovative ways of small actions to reach your goal.

In this third day you will perform and discover how to move forward with your goal and you will find innovative ways of small actions to reach your goal.

Use questions to find goals. I formulate these same questions for me so I find what my goal is.

What can I do?

On this day we create the aptitude and attitude we pursue.

Goals

According to our model we will get our goal.

Movement

This model is based on human behavior and how our conscious and unconscious mind works, this is not a book that seeks to be a scientific thesis or only theoretical work, is a book designed to be practical and immediately applicable

To see results in your life.

Exercise

My goal is this moment is defined so I ask me some questions:

_____

_____

_____

_____

Exercise:

Wednesday:

Questions of my Movement Model – Wednesday

ME Motivation + Entrepreneurship

1. What will be the procedure?

2. Will I get better every day in what I have to do to my goal?

3. Am I motivated enough or should I do something else?

4. What innovations can I create so my goal is met?

5. My high intension is my goal _____

Be fulfilled for _____

6. Do I need more activities for the realization of my goal?

7. Will I try to use some of my innovations?

8. Does my way of proceeding is in line to achieve my goal?

It is important to imagine that the goal is made and go visualizing the goal.

Innovation in terms of what I make. Only you know the steps.

If it is Investigate, read, eat less that day, making a resume, save, in order to innovate in the movement that will approach me to the goal.

Day four: Numbering – To write

In this fourth day we will write the goal that we want to achieve and give it a number. When I say a number I refer to specify when and numbering the steps to take for my goal. Number involves writing, start, terms, dates...

LISTEN TO ME

What are the attributes of the listener?

What do you do when you listen?

What is listening?

It is one of the most difficult skills of human beings because when we hear we understand what our interlocutor is saying and communicating verbally.

Listening is to understand the verbal and nonverbal communication gestures and understanding many movements that want to express something.

I must listen and understand what I'm really doing to achieve my goal.

BEING

Many people focus only on defining what they need to do to have the life they want. Some others believe that first they need to have to determine what to do and be able to define who they are.

When the truth is that first we need to establish who we want to be.

You must keep these 3 questions in your mind: The transformation movement is more than just change what we do, it is based on defining and become who we want and we need TO BE to have the results we're looking for.

The real transformation begins in the BEING, and the changes are durable and sustainable when they are based in the BEING.

Exercise

Fourth day:

NT= Numbering + to write

I must write what I should make to take a move to the goal.

I must write specific dates and specific moves, I will write it in the notebook.

Write even the ideas that come to your mind in the exactly moment that the idea arose.

Questions of the Movement Model

NT Numbering + to write

1. Does the choice of my goal is the right in this moment?

2. What am I going to do today to give effect to my goal?

3. All my energy is balanced in my environment for my other activities?

4. I will number what I have to do every day to the realization of my goal. This is the numbering of the steps and the numbering of the potential dates.

5. I will make this calendar that can be 1 week, 1 month, 3 months, 1 year, 3 years, or more.

Day five:

Friday

The tasks that I will be performing daily are important because they will have a purpose on what will be my goal.

In this fifth day I rectify my organization, my way, I'm numbering and writing. It is important in this phase of the fifth day to bring optimism to its best so that optimism takes me to have a different and innovative attitude on my goal.

In this guide I'll give you some sentences to support your life so it can grow in abundance.

I will imagine a positive fact of my life and feel and make sure that I can achieve it.

I must find a technique to achieve my goal and my activities so I can align it well with my purpose.

My inner technique should develop my external technique.

On this day I have to find what is the relationship with myself and with my goal so I can achieve it.

The positive psychology is very important on this day.

The positive psychology focuses on the study of how to develop positive qualities and helps to live a more fulfilling life and prevent diseases that occur when life seems pointless.

Martin Seligman is the founder of positive psychology. It is important to clarify the difference between positive psychology and positive thinking.

The Positive Psychology is a branch of psychology, and therefore is a science whose conclusions are based on studies and research, and does not advocate that we have to think about the positive daily or deny the reality.

There are moments in which we must have realistic thoughts. In the positive psychology being happy makes more good things in the life of each person occur because happiness makes people get more positive results in all areas of your life and get more satisfying relationships, that is, it's like a multiplier effect where happiness attracts more happiness. If we experience more positive emotions we will live better.

• Positive psychology is defined itself as the science of positive subjective experience, positive individual traits, and positive institutions, it seeks to learn and develop the circumstances that will make flourish individuals, communities and societies.

Beliefs

Our beliefs are determining a high percentage for the criterion in which we will give more importance.

A belief is a feeling of certainty about the meaning of something.

Opportunity

Movement

Belief

We create the beliefs when we acquire experience.

The beliefs will serve me and drive me to become a better person.

We must encourage us to think beyond the known constraints aspirations to think about the aspirations that have weight, that are meaningful, inspiring and suddenly a little uncomfortable.

The aspirations are important.

.They have urgent and important meaning

.They can be imagined in detail, when they are explored in terms of how they look, how they sound and how they feel when you achieve the desired result.

.They create a sense of excitement and anticipation when they are imagined.

.They involve some degree of demand beyond the comfort zone.

Exercise

Friday Fifth day

Phrases

TO Technique + optimism+ Get an answer

1.   I'm going to transform my life to a better level with the movement that I will do for my goal today.

2.   I'm going to use the techniques for my goal, just for me.

3.   I'm going to exploit the occasion that I'm taking to achieve my goal.

4.   It is an opportunity that I have today and if I promised to do a movement today I will do it as an opportunity for succeed in my goal and I will be optimistic.

Day six:

Day six My Focus + Embrace love

Saturday

On day six we will write the strategies that I will use for achieve my goal, specific strategies of movement and with another movement I will do the reinforcement. Today I will do the movement of the sixth day as a new expression of my goal.

I must focus on my goal, so my attention is directed to my goal. Focus and don't lose it. When I say new, I mean to what new movement I can do that will contribute to achieving my goal.

The new things that I do for my movement is a learning experience for my life.

Model

When we have defined our movement model then we have to move to achieve the goal.

Day 1 Monday   M=My goal

O=Organization

Day 2 Tuesday   V=Viable

E= Expectative

Day 3 Wednesday M= Motivation

E= Entrepreneurship +emotions

Day 4 Thursday   N= Numbering

T= to write

S= Start to love

Day 5 friday

I= Illusion+ introduction of priority

N= New technique

Day 6 Saturday

M= My focus

E=Embrace love

Day 7 Sunday

L= Likable attitude

O=Own move

V= Value your movements with responsibility

E= Efficient+ enlarge gratefulness

Movement
When we move is because we are going to take an action relates to our goal and so our goal will become achievable.

When we take responsibility to achieve results it is a way to focus on the responsibility for our lives.

Questions:
The questions are important and for this we must continue according to the guidelines for achieving the goals when we start practicing.

Qualities for a good movement, I must repeat:

- It is okay to make mistakes, because in that way I will learn.
- The people is amazing, all the people – without exception.
- If there is a way to improve and change, I'll find it.
- The movement is measured by the fun that I'm having, the lessons I learn, the help I'm giving to others and the people with whom I connect.
- There are practical or spiritual solutions for everything. Everything has a solution.
- There is always a way to accomplish what I propose.
- If I persist I'll make it.

- When I feel against the wall or in a crisis that's when my best blooms
- There is always a way.
- My sales will be optimal.

- I'm the most motivated seller of the world.
- Selling is an art.
- The job of selling benefits so many people, including me.

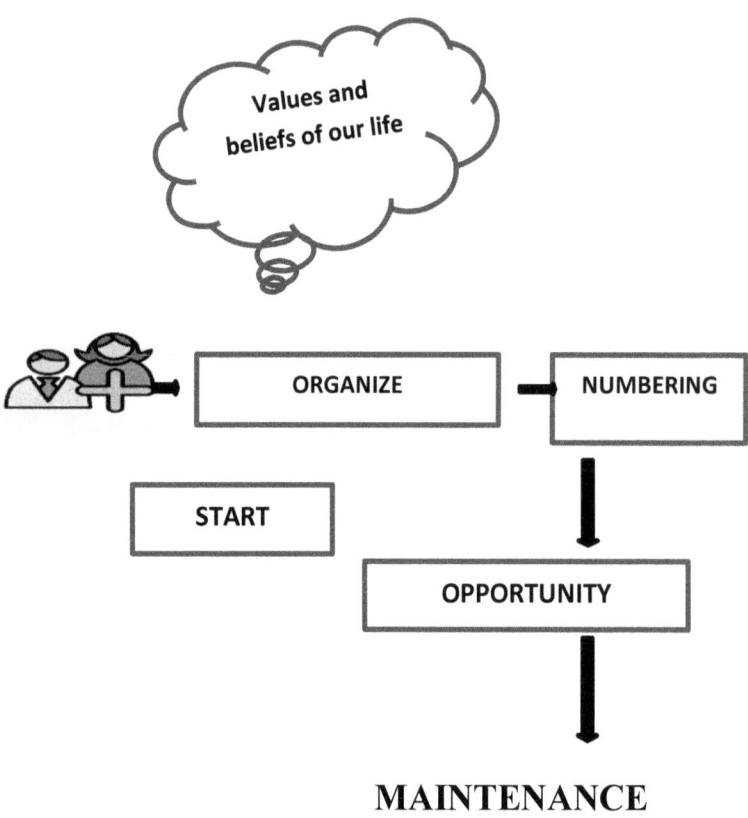

MAINTENANCE

Summing

Seed in me

My notes

_____

_____

_____

_____

_____

_____

_____

_____

Exercise Saturday: My Focus

I'll write on my calendar all I'm doing for my goal, all I'm doing for my mind.

It is my responsibility to check on me what I'm doing for my goal. I gather the positive and I do a review of it to see if I'm getting results.

1. I have to focus on questions so I can analyze every goal.

2. The new things and my daily movements take me to my goal.

3. Focus is the most important thing and I must be commitment to achieve the goal by following the schedule I'll write.

4. Review what I've done to improve or continue in the same way.

5. The focus on my goal is not going to decline

START TO LOVE

Likable Attitude

Own Movement

Value your movements with responsability

Enlarge gratefulness and efficient

I mean I love all the movements of my life.

I appreciate the opportunity to make positive and accurate movements for the realization of the goal.

The responsibility and commitment to carry out the goal and the model are important to everything that relates to bringing life to another level.

Day Seven: Start to LOVE

On this seventh day I start to LOVE, which means Attitude, Movement and Gratitude, where my new attitude will make me take the right move so the action of today will make me advance to my goal.

Because I like so much my goal, I always want to take it to another level and every day I like the most the way I'm performing my goal and I also like the model I'm following.

On this day the most important thing is my responsibility to the accomplishment of my goal and, if my responsibility is in a high degree, I will continue with the movement of my first week during the next weeks. But if I want to impulse myself with my goal I must follow the movement model of the second week.

To Love

On this day we have already identified our goal and we're working and operating for this to become real. We maintain the changes and the transformation identified for our success and for the people that is around us.

My goal should have the opportunity to be loved.

Summing

Seed in me

Notes

_____

_____
_____
_____
_____
_____

Exercise Movement Model

Exercise

Movement Model

Choose an area of your life that is in your mind in this moment. It may be because it is a problem or a challenge, or it may be something exciting and positive. Make sure that is something that you have control and influence.

1, Write a sentence that describes the situation

_____

_____

_____

_____

_____

_____

Examples of goals to follow in sales:

- This year I will be the best seller of my company

- I'm going to start my own business

- I'm going to save more many with my sales

- I need some spiritual practice

- I'm going to leave the bad habits that don't let me be a good seller

- I'm going to learn a new language

- A specific job that I want

- Prepare a holiday

- I want to study courses and seminars to increase my knowledge in sales.

- I want to learn how to motivate my work team

- Work projects

- Health, physical condition and well-being

- Personal growth

- Professional training

- Domestic economy

- Friends, couple and family

- Relationships with customers and partners

Movement

Movement

1.   What is happening right now, what is telling you that this is important to you?

_____

_____

_____

_____

2.   What are you missing?

_____

_____

_____

_____

1. Numbering of ideas to achieve the goal

_____

_____

_____

_____

2. What to do to make your movement and your goal will be fulfilled?

_____

_____

_____

_____

_____

Exercise: Movement In Me

-What are my beliefs in this moment?

_____

_____

_____

_____

_____

_____

What are your opportunities?

_____

_____

_____

_____

What would I like to happen?

_____

_____

_____

_____

_____

_____

My movement and compliance is?

_____

_____

_____

_____

_____

_____

What is my transformation?

_____

_____

_____

_____

_____

_____

What will happen when my goal is complete?

_____

_____

_____

_____

_____

_____

Conclusion

I hope that you can practice the models to have a better planning of the sales.

I wish you the most motivated and successful sales.

Bibliography

Hanan, Mack, James j. Cribbin y Herman Heiser. Consulative Selling. Nueva York: AMACOM 1973.

Raux, Emille. Handbook of Successful New Sales Ideas. Nueva York: Castle Books, n.d.

• Seligman, M. E. P y Csikszentmihalyi, M. (2000),"positive psychology: an introduction", American Psychologist.

• Cayrol, A, y J. de Saint – Paul: Mente sin límites: la PNL, Barcelona, Paidós Ibérica, 1992 (3ª ed).

• Programación neurolingüística cambie su vida con PNL (Dr Roderich Heinze. Sabine Vohmann – Heinze.

KOTLER, P.: Dirección de mercadotecnia, 2.ª ed., México: Diana, 1974.

THANKS!

Thank you for purchasing this eBook.

If you enjoyed this eBook, please consider leaving a brief review with Amazon.com and share the link with friends and favorite places social media.

Again, thank you!